A TRUE BOOK™

My United States

Kentucky

JENNIFER ZEIGER

Children's Press®
An Imprint of Scholastic Inc.

Content Consultant

James Wolfinger, PhD, Associate Dean and Professor
College of Education, DePaul University, Chicago, Illinois

Library of Congress Cataloging-in-Publication Data
Names: Zeiger, Jennifer, author.
Title: Kentucky / by Jennifer Zeiger.
Description: New York, NY : Children's Press, an imprint of Scholastic Inc., 2018. | Series: A true book | Includes
bibliographical references and index.
Identifiers: LC CN 2017045275 | ISBN 9780531231654 (library binding) | ISBN 9780531247167 (pbk.)
Subjects: LCSH: Kentucky—Juvenile literature.
Classification: LCC F451.3 .Z45 2018 | DDC 976.9—dc23
LC record available at https://lccn.loc.gov/2017045275

All rights reserved. Published in 2018 by Children's Press, an imprint of Scholastic Inc.
Printed in North Mankato, MN, USA 113

Scholastic Inc., 557 Broadway, New York, NY 10012

1 2 3 4 5 6 7 8 9 10 R 27 26 25 24 23 22 21 20 19 18

Front cover: Kentucky Derby

Back cover: Louisville Slugger factory

Welcome to Kentucky

Find the Truth!

Everything you are about to read is true *except* for one of the sentences on this page.

Which one is **TRUE**?

T or F Kentucky fought on the side of the South in the Civil War.

T or F Kentucky has had four state capitols.

UNITED STATES

Kentucky

Find the answers in this book.

Contents

THE **BIG** TRUTH!

Blackberry

What Represents Kentucky?

4

Cardinal

Newport Aquarium

Thoroughbred

This Is Kentucky!

INDIANA

OHIO

N W E S

0 — 50
Miles

ILLINOIS

1 Kentucky Derby at Churchill Downs

The Knobs

COVINGTON

Ohio

FRANKFORT

Fort Knox

Fort Boonesborough State Park

Ohio River

Ohio

LOUISVILLE

LEXINGTON

Kentucky

OWENSBORO

KENTUCKY

Berea College

Black Mountain

Mountain

Mammoth Cave

BOWLING GREEN

Fisher-Ridge Cave

Cumberland

2

Appalachian

4

Mississippi

Kentucky Lake

Mississippi River

Trail of Tears Commemorative Park

Daniel Boone National Forest

Tallest Tree in Kentucky

Cumberland Gap National Historical Park

3

Appalachian Mountains

CUMBERLAND GAP

MISSOURI

TENNESSEE

1 Churchill Downs Racetrack

This is the home of America's most famous horse race, the Kentucky Derby. More than a million people attend the two-week festival leading up to the Derby each year.

② Daniel Boone National Forest

This national forest was named after one of Kentucky's most famous pioneers. From boating and fishing to climbing and camping, the forest offers something for just about every outdoor adventurer.

③ Cumberland Gap National Historical Park

From deep caves to high mountains, this national park is full of natural beauty. It's also the site of a historic mountain pass through which people have traveled for thousands of years.

④ Black Mountain

As the state's highest peak, Black Mountain offers a beautiful view of the surrounding countryside. This mountain has also played an important part in Kentucky's coal-mining history.

Despite its name, the famous Kentucky bluegrass is actually a rich shade of green.

CHAPTER 1

Land and Wildlife

Kentucky is a land defined by tall mountains and deep caves. Travel north to see gentle rolling hills. Go west, and you can explore wetlands filled with wildlife. The Ohio River traces a snaking northern border. The Mississippi River loops along the state's southwestern side. The Kentucky, Cumberland, and other rivers flow into and out of Kentucky's interior. Lakes—some long and deep, others small and shallow—dot the landscape.

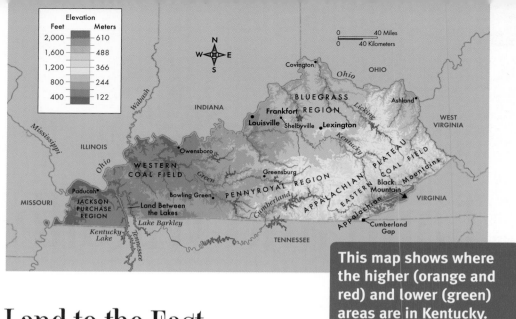

This map shows where the higher (orange and red) and lower (green) areas are in Kentucky.

Land to the East

In the eastern quarter of Kentucky lie mountains, including the state's highest peak, Black Mountain. They are part of the long chain of Appalachian Mountains. Kentucky's Eastern Coal Field, a major source of U.S. coal, is found in these highlands. The Appalachian **Plateau** lies just west of the mountains. Cutting through the mountains to the plateau beyond, you can find the famous Cumberland Gap. People have long taken this pass between peaks to travel west.

Mammoth Cave

As the world's longest cave system, central Kentucky's Mammoth Cave is truly "mammoth." More than 400 miles (644 kilometers) of it are mapped, but it extends beyond this. People first explored and mined the cave thousands of years ago. Kentuckians have led tours through the system for more than 200 years. Today, visitors can see many fantastic sights, including cave formations in the shapes of waterfalls and flowers, and cave species found nowhere else in the world.

Kentucky is home to two of the world's longest caves: Mammoth Cave and the Fisher-Ridge cave system.

Horses are a common sight on Kentucky farms.

Land to the West

The hilly Bluegrass region lies in northern Kentucky, west of the plateau. It is named for the bluegrass that thrives in its fields. The horse farms here are particularly famous. To the south, the Pennyroyal region is named after the species of mint called pennyroyal found there. Cliffs, **gorges**, and caves are scattered through this land. In the Western Coal Field region, farming and mining exist side by side. Kentucky's westernmost corner is Jackson Purchase. Fertile farmland and wetlands fill this small region.

What's the Forecast?

Kentucky enjoys fairly mild temperatures. The weather is neither extremely hot in summer nor extremely cold in winter. Though the temperatures are moderate, the rain is not, especially in the south. Floods often create problems. Earthquakes are another threat. Kentucky is part of the New Madrid Fault zone, where quakes are rare but extreme. From 1811 to 1812, the state experienced a series of earthquakes so intense that the Mississippi River looked like it was flowing backward.

A worker prepares a car to be pulled out of an area that was flooded by an overflowing creek.

MAXIMUM TEMPERATURE
114°F

MINIMUM TEMPERATURE
-37°F

Natural Bridge State Park is named for an amazing rock formation that visitors can walk across.

A Walk in the Forest

About half of Kentucky is covered in forests, and they include a range of trees. Oak, chestnut, cedar, and maple trees are just a few that grow here. Some, such as the dogwood and yellow poplar, bloom with beautiful flowers each spring. Pines and other evergreens grow high up in the mountains. Along Kentucky's many waterways, bald cypresses and other water-loving trees thrive.

Animals

Kentucky is home to a huge variety of animals. Hundreds of birds are found in the state. Some, such as cardinals and blue jays, add a splash of color to the forest. The graceful blue heron and other **migrating** birds pass through Kentucky on their way north or south.

Small mammals fill the forests, including rabbits, woodchucks, and squirrels. Deer and elk search for plants to eat. In some places, bison even roam.

Sandhill cranes are among the many birds that pass through Kentucky as part of their migration each year.

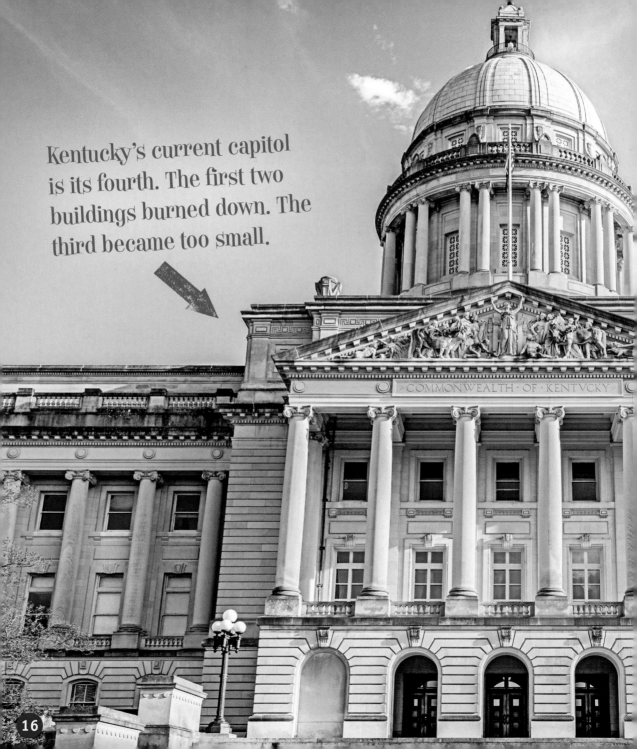

Kentucky's current capitol is its fourth. The first two buildings burned down. The third became too small.

COMMONWEALTH · OF · KENTVCKY

CHAPTER 2

Government

Frankfort has been Kentucky's capital since 1792, when Kentucky became a state. But throughout the 19th century, many government officials tried to move the capital to Louisville or Lexington. Both cities have always been much bigger than Frankfort. Despite gaining a lot of support within the government and from the people, no one has succeeded in moving the state seat out of Frankfort.

Local Government

Kentucky's state government is divided into three branches. The legislative branch writes the state's laws. The governor oversees the executive branch, which enforces those laws. The courts make up the judicial branch and interpret the state's laws.

KENTUCKY'S STATE GOVERNMENT

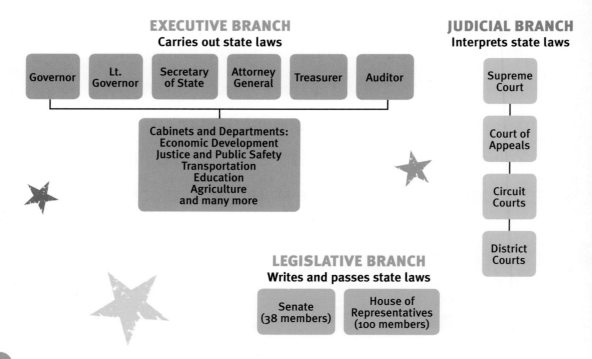

EXECUTIVE BRANCH
Carries out state laws

| Governor | Lt. Governor | Secretary of State | Attorney General | Treasurer | Auditor |

Cabinets and Departments:
Economic Development
Justice and Public Safety
Transportation
Education
Agriculture
and many more

JUDICIAL BRANCH
Interprets state laws

Supreme Court

Court of Appeals

Circuit Courts

District Courts

LEGISLATIVE BRANCH
Writes and passes state laws

Senate (38 members)

House of Representatives (100 members)

Deciding Vote

Kentucky's governor is powerful. In most states, the governor can't appoint people to top-level government positions without approval from

A police officer on horseback helps keep the peace at a rally for President Donald Trump in Louisville.

the legislative branch. The same is true for the U.S. government. In Kentucky, however, the governor needs no approval for a lot of state government jobs. This gives the governor more power over what happens in many executive departments.

 With this much power, the choice of governor is an important one. So at election time, many Kentuckians carefully consider who will get their vote for governor.

Kentucky in the National Government

Each state elects officials to represent it in the U.S. Congress. Like every state, Kentucky has two senators. The U.S. House of Representatives relies on a state's population to determine its numbers. Kentucky has six representatives in the House.

Every four years, states vote on the next U.S. president. Each state is granted a number of electoral votes based on its number of members in Congress. With two senators and six representatives, Kentucky has eight electoral votes.

2 senators and 6 representatives

8 electoral votes

With eight electoral votes, Kentucky's voice in presidenti elections is about average.

Representing Kentucky

Elected officials in Kentucky represent a population with a range of interests, lifestyles, and backgrounds.

Ethnicity (2016 estimates)

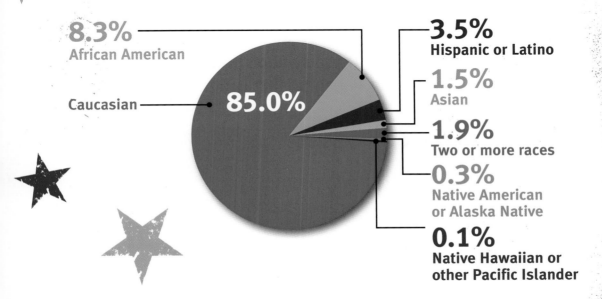

8.3%
African American

Caucasian

85.0%

3.5%
Hispanic or Latino

1.5%
Asian

1.9%
Two or more races

0.3%
Native American or Alaska Native

0.1%
Native Hawaiian or other Pacific Islander

70% live in cities.

5.1% speak a language other than English at home.

22.3% of the population have a degree beyond high school.

84.2% of the population graduated from high school.

67.2% own their own homes.

What Represents Kentucky?

States choose specific animals, plants, and objects to represent the values and characteristics of the land and its people. Find out why these symbols were chosen to represent Kentucky or discover surprising curiosities about them.

Flag

The state flag has the same gold and blue of the seal, and the seal is at the center.

Seal

At the center of Kentucky's seal are two friends shaking hands. The formally dressed man on the right represents England's colonial presence in the region. The man on the left represents Kentucky's pioneers.

Cardinal

STATE BIRD

Unlike many other birds, cardinals do not migrate or lose their bright colors during winter.

Appalachian Dulcimer

STATE INSTRUMENT

A musician usually sets this instrument on his or her lap and plucks its strings to play it.

Freshwater Pearl

STATE GEMSTONE

Different species of mussels create different colors and shapes of freshwater pearls in pearl farms along Kentucky Lake.

Thoroughbred

STATE HORSE

Thoroughbreds were developed specifically to be racehorses. They are fast and good at jumping.

Blackberry

STATE FRUIT

These little fruits are also called brambleberries, thimbleberries, and dewberries.

Goldenrod

STATE FLOWER

Goldenrods appear on both the state seal and the flag of Kentucky.

America was once home to 30 million to 60 million wild bison. Many of them roamed through Kentucky's meadows.

CHAPTER 3

History

Where did the name *Kentucky* come from? No one can quite agree. It may be related to what Native American groups called the area, whether "land of tomorrow" or "land of meadows." European settlers in later centuries knew the region as Kentucke or Cantucky, but they didn't know why.

However its name came about, Kentucky was known as a land of rolling hills, flowing waters, and beauty. This land has been home to many people over thousands of years.

Native Americans

The first Kentuckians came as early as 12,000 years ago. These Paleo-Indians were hunters and gatherers. They killed giant bison, mammoths, and other animals for meat. They also searched for herbs, roots, berries, and other edible plants.

Over time, people developed ways to farm. They grew squash, gourds, and sunflowers. Communities often grew more than they needed. They traded extra goods with people as far away as the Great Lakes and the Gulf of Mexico.

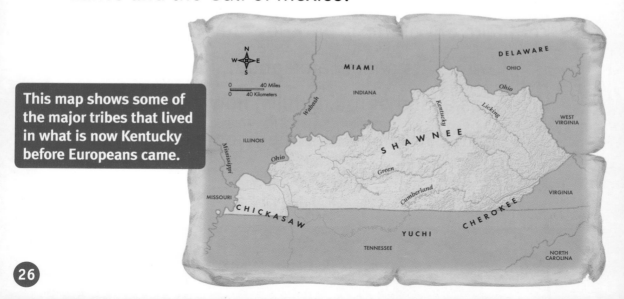

This map shows some of the major tribes that lived in what is now Kentucky before Europeans came.

Among the most recent native groups in Kentucky were the Shawnee, Cherokee, and Chickasaw. The Shawnee once lived across much of central Kentucky. They farmed crops during the spring and summer. They also tapped maple trees to collect sap and turn

A Shawnee woman

it into syrup. In colder months, they traveled and hunted. The Cherokee lived in the southeast along the Appalachian Mountains. The Chickasaw were to the southwest. Both groups farmed and lived in permanent villages.

Europeans

The first Europeans to spy what is now Kentucky were French explorers in 1673, but they didn't stay. It wasn't until the 1700s that Europeans became really interested in Kentucky. In 1749, French explorer Pierre-Joseph Céloron de Blainville claimed the region as France's territory. Just one year later, a group led by Thomas Walker traveled through the Cumberland Gap. They explored the land for the British **colony** of Virginia.

This map shows routes European explorers took as they explored and settled what is now Kentucky.

Jolliet and Marquette, 1673
Thomas Walker, 1750
John Finley, 1752
Daniel Boone, 1769, 1775
Mounds
Fort
Early settlement
Present-day state of Kentucky

N
W E
S

Mississippi
Ohio
Wabash
Ohio
Kentucky
Licking
Kanawha
Louisville
Lexington
Bardstown
Boonesborough
Harrodsburg
Logan's Station
Wilderness Road
Green
Wickliffe Mounds
Cumberland
Cumberland Gap

0   40 Miles
0   40 Kilometers

Kentucky's Native Americans often lived in homes made from wood, animal skins, and other natural materials.

Colonists started to trickle into the area. The first were hunters looking for beavers and other animals that had valuable **pelts**. In 1775, Daniel Boone cut the Wilderness Trail from the Cumberland Gap to the Bluegrass region. This made travel easier.

Most of the new settlers were white. Some free black people also came. Many, however, were slaves. By 1777, slaves made up about ten percent of the population.

Becoming Kentucky

During and after the Revolutionary War (1775–1783), Kentucky was a **county** in Virginia. But Kentuckians were not happy with Virginia's government. The capital in Richmond was difficult to reach. People also felt that Virginian officials did not pay much attention to Kentucky. Between 1784 and 1792, Kentucky representatives outlined their own state government. Their plan was approved, and Kentucky became the 15th U.S. state on June 1, 1792.

Timeline of Kentucky Events

1673 CE
French explorers become the first Europeans to visit Kentucky.

10,000 BCE ➤ **1673 CE** ➤ **1792**

10,000 BCE
People arrive in what is now Kentucky for the first time.

June 1, 1792
Kentucky becomes the 15th state.

Major Changes

In 1818, General Andrew Jackson bought what later became known as the Jackson Purchase from the Chickasaw. Beginning in 1838, native groups were forced to leave Kentucky.

During the Civil War (1861-1865), Kentucky tried to stay out of the fight between the free North and the slaveholding South. But when Southern troops invaded the state, Kentuckians entered the war on the Union side.

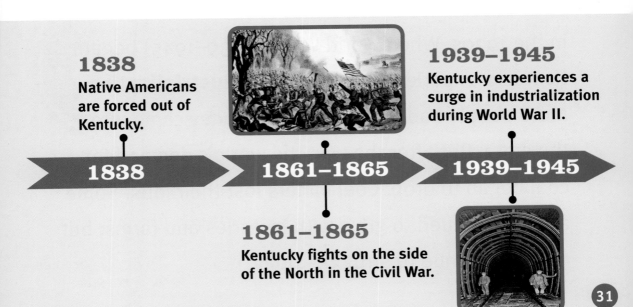

1838
Native Americans are forced out of Kentucky.

1939–1945
Kentucky experiences a surge in industrialization during World War II.

1838   **1861–1865**   **1939–1945**

1861–1865
Kentucky fights on the side of the North in the Civil War.

Coal miners ride out of a mine in Cumberland after a long shift of work.

More Modern Times

Kentucky's economy struggled to recover after the Civil War. The Great Depression made matters worse in the 1930s. When World War II (1939–1945) began, Kentucky experienced a surge in **industrialization**. More people had jobs, and more money came into the state. But after the war, the world's demand for coal began to drop. Coal miners lost their jobs. Some areas continued to grow with factories and farms, but others continue to struggle today.

Prizefighter

Muhammad Ali was born Cassius Clay Jr. in Louisville in 1942. One of the greatest boxers in history, he was also a fierce **activist**. He often spoke out about equal rights. He changed his name to Muhammad Ali when he converted to Islam in 1964. As a Muslim, Ali firmly believed in peace. When the U.S. Army **drafted** him during the Vietnam War (1954– 1975), he refused to go. Because of this, Ali lost his boxing title and was not allowed to fight for more than three years.

Newport Aquarium's shark tank holds 850,000 gallons (3.2 million liters) of water!

CHAPTER 4

Culture

The rivers, grasses, forests, and mountains of Kentucky have defined more than the state's landscape. They have also shaped the people who live there. Poets and novelists have written of the state's coal miners, farmers, and landmarks. John James Audubon, the famous **naturalist**, found inspiration outside Louisville before publishing his sketches in *The Birds of America* in the mid-1800s. The plant life has even given its name to Kentucky's most famous music: bluegrass, a style of country music developed in the 1940s.

Sports and Recreation

Kentucky doesn't have any professional sports teams. Fans do, however, cheer on their college and even high school teams. They especially love to watch the University of Kentucky Wildcats and the University of Louisville Cardinals. The biggest draw is college basketball, and for good reason. The University of Kentucky's team has won eight NCAA championships! Football is also very popular.

The University of Louisville Cardinals take the field during a home game.

A bluegrass group performs in front of the International Bluegrass Music Museum in Owensboro.

Celebrations

A great way to get a taste of Kentucky is to sample the state's festivals. Food fans travel to Owensboro for the International Bar-B-Q Festival and to London for the World Chicken Festival. Music buffs head to the Festival of the Bluegrass in Lexington. The Kentucky Derby is a chance for major celebration, as food and fun fill Louisville for days before the big race.

Work

Farming has always been a big part of Kentucky's economy. It is particularly important in the Jackson Purchase region. Manufacturing, however, provides a larger part of the state's income. Food processing, appliance manufacturing, and printing are a few examples. Most people work some sort of service job. This includes people who work in hotels and restaurants. Many service workers are employed at the state's two big military bases, Fort Knox and Fort Campbell.

Kentucky has almost 13 million acres (5.2 million hectares) of farmland.

Working in the Coal Mine

Coal was once a huge moneymaker for Kentucky. It was a common source of fuel. Burning coal, however, releases harmful **pollutants** into the air. During the 20th century, people started using less coal to cut down on the pollution. Coal companies struggled as a result. Miners lost their jobs, and the state suffered. Over the decades, manufacturing and service jobs have replaced much of Kentucky's coal-mining income. The transition, however, has been difficult. Manufacturing jobs are only available in certain areas, and many coal-mining regions remain in economic trouble.

Barges haul coal up the Ohio River near Louisville.

Taste Test

Kentucky food is more than just fried chicken. Burgoo is a stew that is traditionally created for big gatherings. It includes meat and vegetables, and every chef has his or her own recipe. Hoppin' John, another tasty dish, is a mix of black-eyed peas and rice.

  ## Easy Burgoo Stew

Ask an adult to help you!

Ingredients

2–3 pounds total of three different kinds of meat (chicken, pork, beef, etc.)
salt
1 green pepper, chopped
2 large onions, chopped
2 cloves garlic, chopped
1 14.5-ounce can diced tomatoes
1–2 cups each of your favorite fresh and frozen vegetables

1 bay leaf
1/2 teaspoon black pepper
1/2 teaspoon thyme
2 cups chicken stock
1 large red-skinned potato cut into pieces
1 tablespoon cornstarch
1/4 cup water

Directions

With an adult's help, dice the meat and brown it in a pan, salting it as it cooks. Combine the meat, green pepper, onions, garlic, tomatoes, fresh vegetables, spices, and stock in a slow cooker. Add the potatoes on top. Cover and cook on low for 6 hours. Stir in the frozen vegetables. Cook for another 30 minutes to 1 hour. Combine the cornstarch and water in a separate container. Stir this into the stew and let cook, uncovered, for 10 minutes.

Children play in a fountain in downtown Louisville.

Beautiful Kentucky

A state as rich in culture and natural beauty as Kentucky is truly worth experiencing. There is something for everyone. Music lovers can tap their feet to bluegrass tunes, and sports fans can catch a college game. Those who love the outdoors can walk through forests or hike up mountains. Looking for excitement? Try the Kentucky Derby. Would you rather explore? There are countless cave systems. For residents and visitors alike, Kentucky is a great state! ★

Famous People

Daniel Boone

(1734–1820) was a frontiersman whose adventures made him a legendary figure in American history. He was one of the first Europeans to explore Kentucky.

Abraham Lincoln

(1809–1865) was the 16th president of the United States. He was assassinated in 1865, near the end of the Civil War. He was born on a farm in Kentucky.

Kit Carson

(1809–1868) was a soldier and explorer who helped settle the American West. He was born in Richmond.

Colonel Harland Sanders

(1890–1980) was the founder of the Kentucky Fried Chicken fast-food chain. He lived in Louisville.

Bill Monroe

(1911–1996) was a singer, songwriter, and musician. He was a pioneer in the style of music called bluegrass. Monroe grew up on a farm in Kentucky.

Whitney M. Young Jr.

(1921–1971) fought against employment discrimination during the civil rights movement of the 1950s and 1960s. He was born in Shelby County.

Loretta Lynn

(1932–) is one of the most acclaimed singer-songwriters in country music history. She is from Butcher Hollow.

Jennifer Lawrence

(1990–) is an actress who has appeared in many films, including *The Hunger Games* series. She was born in Indian Hills.

Diane Sawyer

(1945–) is a television news anchor who has appeared on shows such as *Good Morning America* and *Primetime*. She was born in Glasgow.

George Clooney

(1961–) is an award-winning actor and filmmaker who has starred in films such as *Ocean's Eleven* (2001) and *Gravity* (2013). He is from Lexington.

Did You Know That...

There's one small part of Kentucky that is entirely cut off from the rest of the state: Kentucky Bend. This section of land is attached to Tennessee and surrounded on all other sides by the Mississippi River, but it is part of Kentucky.

A moonbow is a rainbow in a waterfall's mist that is created by the light of the moon. Kentucky's Cumberland Falls is one place to see one.

During the Civil War, both sides had their own presidents. Abraham Lincoln was head of the United States in the North. Jefferson Davis was elected president of the Confederacy in the South. Lincoln and Davis were born less than one year and 100 miles (160 km) apart in Kentucky (Lincoln in Hodgenville and Davis in Fairview).

Kentucky's Dinosaur World theme park is home to hundreds of life-sized dinosaur sculptures.

There are more miles of running water in Kentucky than in any other U.S. state except Alaska.

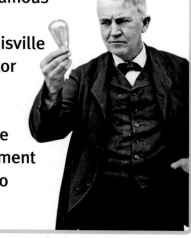

Thomas Edison, the famous inventor, worked for Western Union in Louisville as a telegraph operator in the 1860s. He was fired after he spilled acid in the office while conducting an experiment that had nothing to do with his work.

The song "Happy Birthday" was first written as "Good Morning to All" by teachers in Kentucky.

Did you find the truth?

F Kentucky fought on the side of the South in the Civil War.

T Kentucky has had four state capitols.

Resources

Books

Nonfiction

Gregory, Josh. *Muhammad Ali*. New York: Children's Press, 2017.

Santella, Andrew. *Kentucky*. New York: Children's Press, 2014.

Fiction

Morrison, Toni. *Beloved*. New York: Knopf, 1987.

Tevis, Walter. *The Man Who Fell to Earth*. Boston: Gregg Press, 1963.

Visit this Scholastic website for more information on Kentucky:

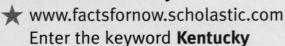 www.factsfornow.scholastic.com
Enter the keyword **Kentucky**

Important Words

activist (AK-tuh-vist) a person who works to bring about social or political change

colony (KAH-luh-nee) a territory that has been settled by people from another country and is controlled by that country

county (KOWN-tee) a division of a state with its own local government

drafted (DRAF-tid) made to join the armed forces

gorges (GOR-jiz) deep valleys or ravines

industrialization (in-dus-tree-uh-lih-ZAY-shuhn) the process of building more factories and making things in large quantities

migrating (MYE-gray-ting) moving to another area or climate at a particular time of year

naturalist (NATCH-ur-uh-list) someone who studies plants, animals, and other living things

pelts (PELTS) skins from an animal with the hair or fur still on them

plateau (pla-TOH) an area of level ground that is higher than the surrounding area

pollutants (puh-LOO-tuhnts) substances that contaminate another substance

Index

Page numbers in **bold** indicate illustrations.

About the Author

Jennifer Zeiger is an editor and author living in Chicago, Illinois. She has written several nonfiction books on a range of topics, from history to science. A lifelong lover of caves, she hopes to explore Mammoth Cave someday soon!